WHALES

BY DAN GREENBERG

BENCHMARK **B**OOKS

MARSHALL CAVENDISH
NEW YORK

Series Consultant
James Doherty
General Curator
Bronx Zoo, New York

Benchmark Books
Marshall Cavendish Corporation
99 White Plains Road
Tarrytown, NY 10591-9001

Library of Congress Cataloging-in-Publication data:
Greenberg, Daniel A.
Whales / by Dan Greenberg.
p. cm.
Includes index (p. 48).
Summary: Examines the physical characteristics, behavior, and habitat of whales and describes different types.
ISBN 0-7614-1167-4
1. Whales–Juvenile literature. [1. Whales.] I. Title
QL737.C4   G74   2000
599.5–dc21   00-024390

Cover photo: *Animals, Animals* / Zig Leszczynski

All photographs are used by permission and through the courtesy of Animals, Animals: Johnny Johnson, 1, 17, 32, 43; James Watt, 7, 8, 13, 24, 36; Zig Leszczynski, 10; T. Martin, 14, 28, 41; E. R. Degginger, 15; Stefano Nicolini, 16; Henry Ausloos, 20; Ralph Reinhold, 27 (top); Richard Sobol, 27 (bottom), 42; Shane Moore, 30; T. Borrill, 33; D. Allan, 38.

Printed in Hong Kong

3 5 6 4 2

CONTENTS

1
INTRODUCING WHALES

Whales are the largest animals on Earth. The biggest whale of all, the blue whale, is larger than any animal ever known. It is longer than the tallest giraffe. It is heavier than the heftiest hippo. Side by side, the blue whale would make even the greatest of the dinosaurs look small.

How big is a blue whale? Its heart is the size of a small car. Its blood vessels are as wide as drainpipes. The largest land animal, the elephant, could stand on a blue whale's tongue!

Whales, along with dolphins and

A HUMPBACK WHALE SPY-HOPPING OFF THE COAST OF ADMIRALTY ISLAND IN ALASKA. MANY DIFFERENT KINDS OF WHALES RAISE THEIR HEADS ABOVE THE WATER LIKE THIS.

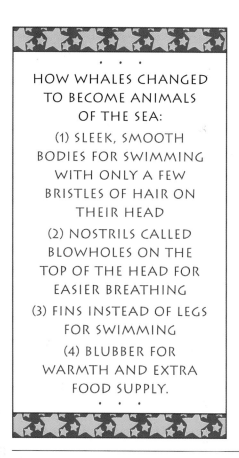
porpoises, belong to a group of animals called *cetaceans*. Cetaceans live in every ocean on Earth. At first glance, you might mistake cetaceans for fish. But they are *mammals*.

How do we know that whales are mammals and not fish? First, like all mammals, whales are *warm-blooded*. Fish are *cold-blooded*. Second, like other mammals, whales breathe air through lungs, while fish take in water through *gills* to breathe.

NOTICE THE SIZE OF THE BLUE WHALE AND ITS BABY COMPARED TO THE HUMAN BEING. BLUE WHALES ARE THE LARGEST ANIMALS LIVING ON THIS PLANET.

AS THIS SOUTHERN RIGHT WHALE MAKES A DIVE IT DISPLAYS ITS MAGNIFICENT TAIL.

Finally, whales give birth to live babies that drink their mother's milk. Fish give birth to live young or lay eggs that may take a few weeks to hatch. Their mothers do not feed them.

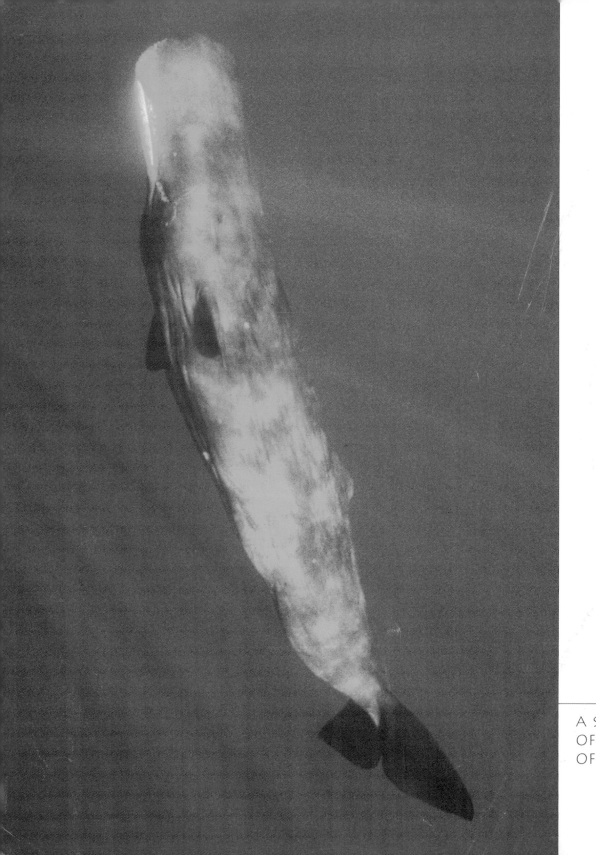

A SPERM WHALE
OFF THE COAST
OF HAWAII.

Most mammals live on land. How did whales come to live underwater? The first cetaceans were actually very small and lived near the mouths of rivers. Gradually, these creatures moved farther and farther out to sea. Over millions of years, their body form changed. Eventually, they became whales, the giant mammals of the ocean.

How big is a blue whale?
The largest living land animal is the African elephant. To match the length of a 100-foot (30 meter) blue whale, eight elephants would need to line up end to end. One of the largest land animals that ever lived is Diplodocus, a dinosaur. The blue whale is still about 10 feet (3 meters) longer than Diplodocus, and would outweigh it by more than 100 tons.

MALE AND FEMALE
BELUGAS, OR
WHITE WHALES.

2
DIFFERENT TYPES OF WHALES

Scientists have organized the many different types of whales in a special way. First, they divide whales into two main groups, or suborders—toothed whales and baleen whales. Within each suborder there are different families, and within each family there may be several different *species*, or kinds, of whales.

Toothed whales include killer whales, beaked whales, and the mighty sperm whale. Toothed whales are hunters. They use their teeth to catch fish, squid, and other sea animals. All whales have *blowholes*, nostrils on the top of their head, for breathing.

A PILOT WHALE WITH A DIVER OFF THE COAST OF HAWAII. PILOT WHALES ARE TOOTHED WHALES.

NARWHAL WHALES LIVE IN
COLDER, MORE NORTHERLY
WATERS THAN ANY OTHER
WHALE. THE NARWHAL HAS A
LONG TUSK AND IS SOMETIMES
CALLED THE UNICORN WHALE.

14

Baleen whales have two blowholes, while toothed whales have only one. All whales live in groups called *pods*. Pods of toothed whales stay close together, helping each other hunt and care for their young. Baleen whales tend to be loners, swimming in pods that are much more spread out.

Baleen whales include right whales, humpback whales, and the biggest cetacean of them all, the blue whale. Baleen whales don't have teeth, so they use strainers called *baleen* to collect food. Baleen is made of rows of plates that mesh together. The plates are attached to the upper jaw. Together, they form a furry fringe around the whale's mouth. To get food, baleen whales take in large amounts of water. The whale forces the water out through its baleen, and thousands of tiny shellfish and other creatures are trapped inside.

TOOTHED WHALES,
SUCH AS THIS BELUGA
WHALE, HAVE ONLY
ONE BLOWHOLE.

THIS PAIR OF SOUTHERN RIGHT WHALES IS BASKING IN THE SUN OFF THE COAST OF ARGENTINA, IN SOUTH AMERICA.

. . .

BARNACLES

WHY DO GRAY WHALES AND RIGHT WHALES BECOME COVERED WITH SMALL SHELLED CREATURES CALLED BARNACLES? BARNACLES WILL USUALLY ATTACH TO ANY SLOW-MOVING OR NONMOVING OBJECT. BARNACLES PROBABLY ATTACH TO GRAY AND RIGHT WHALES BECAUSE THEY DON'T SWIM VERY FAST. RORQUAL WHALES AND MOST TOOTHED WHALES THAT MOVE FAST DON'T HAVE BARNACLES.

. . .

Most rorqual whales, one of the families of baleen whales, feed by themselves. But humpbacks, a species of rorqual, sometimes work together, catching fish by "bubble netting." The humpbacks form a circle. One of the whales swims under a school of fish, herding them into a circle by blowing bubbles. Then the whales swoop in and catch the herded fish!

TOOTHED WHALES

SPERM WHALES

3 Species
- Dwarf sperm whale
- Pygmy sperm whale
- Sperm whale

The largest of the toothed whales, the sperm whale is the deepest diver of all whales. It hunts squid, fish, and other prey.

KILLER WHALES

6 Species
- Killer whale
- Pygmy killer whale
- False killer whale
- Melon–headed whale
- Short–finned pilot whale
- Long–finned pilot whale

Killer whales, or orcas, attack and eat fish, birds, and other mammals, including much larger whales. Killer whales hunt in groups.

NARWHAL AND BELUGA

2 Species
- Narwhal
- Beluga

The two species in this family look very different. The narwhal has a long tusk and is often called the unicorn whale. This beluga, or white whale, is very light in color.

BEAKED WHALES

18 Species
- Including:
- Baird's beaked whale
- Cuvier's beaked whale
- Bottlenose whale

Beaked whales are among the oldest forms of cetaceans. This is a bottlenose whale.

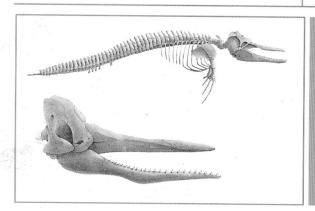

THE SKELETON OF A SPERM WHALE. NOTICE THE ROW OF SHARP TEETH ALONG ITS LOWER JAW.

BALEEN WHALES

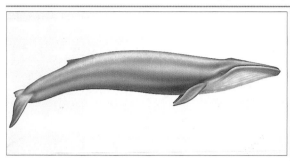

RORQUALS

6 Species
- Blue whale
- Fin whale
- Sei whale
- Bryde's whale
- Minke whale
- Humpback whale

Rorquals, such as the giant blue whale, are fast and sleek. All rorquals have throat grooves. These wrinkles along the throat allow a rorqual's mouth to gulp huge amounts of water.

RIGHT WHALES

4 Species
- Pygmy right whale
- Bowhead
- Northern right whale
- Southern right whale

Right whales like this bowhead are much slower than rorquals. Thick blubber protects bowheads against the cold in the icy waters where they live.

GRAY WHALE

1 Species
- Gray whale

This slow creature gets covered with barnacles as it combs the ocean floor for food. When captured, however, grays can be ferocious fighters.

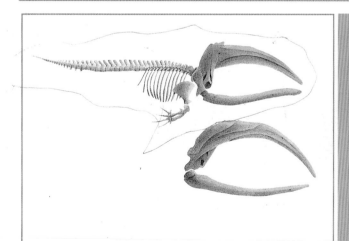

THIS IS THE SKELETON OF A BALEEN WHALE. FROM ITS HUGE, TOOTH-LESS UPPER JAW HANGS THE BALEEN.

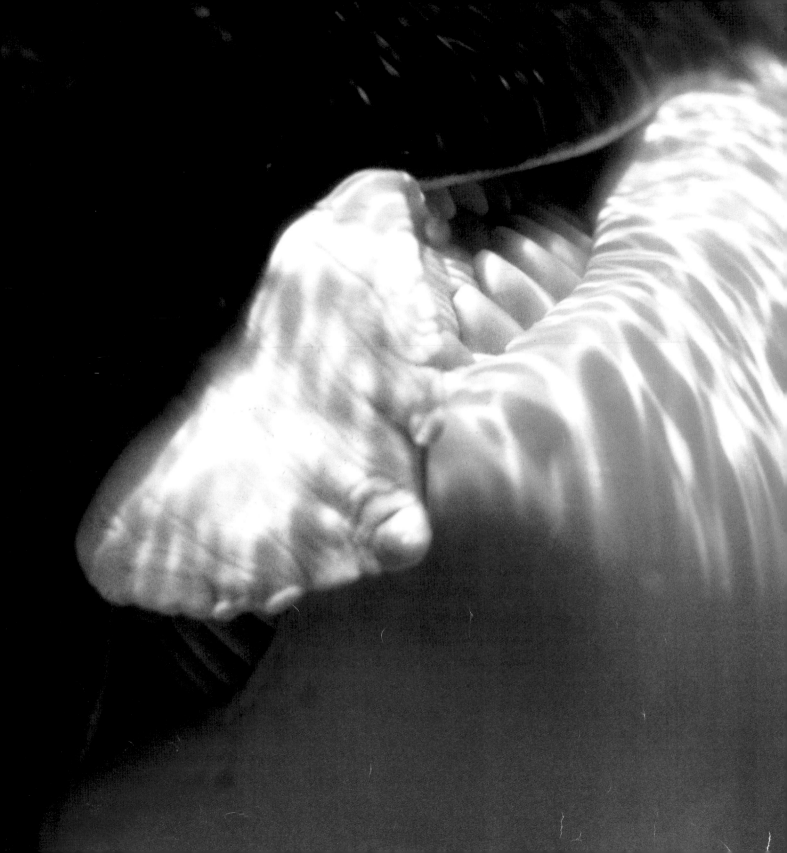

3
WHALES IN ACTION

Whales live in a dark under-water world. Their eyesight is poor. Their sense of smell is weak. So how do they find food? Toothed whales use *echolocation* to find prey. They form a "picture" of their underwater world with sounds, or echoes.

How does echolocation work? First a whale sends out pulses of sound. Then it times how long it takes for the echo to return from an object. The whale uses this information to judge the distance to the object. Using echolocation, toothed whales can tell where fish, squid, and other prey are.

KILLER WHALES USE ECHOLOCATION TO FIND PREY AND THEIR SHARP TEETH TO CATCH IT.

Baleen whales do not seem to have echolocation systems. Instead, these *filter feeders* take in food either by skimming or gulping large amounts of water. Skimmers, like the slow-moving right whale, swim along with their mouth open. As they take in water, skimmers filter food through their baleen. They let the water out of another part of their mouth.

Did you know that sound travels five times as fast underwater as it does in the air? This speed helps whales use echolocation to sense their surroundings very quickly. Some scientists even think that sperm whales might use strong sound waves to stun their prey.

THE BOWHEAD IS OFTEN A SURFACE FEEDER. IT CRUISES ALONG SLOWLY WITH ITS MOUTH OPEN, FILTERING SHRIMP AND OTHER PREY THROUGH ITS FINE CURTAIN OF BALEEN.

Gulpers are the faster-moving *rorquals*. A blue whale, the largest rorqual, can take in 66 tons of water in a single gulp. The whale then uses its immense tongue to push the water out of its mouth through the baleen. This traps fish, shrimplike krill, and other prey against the fringe of baleen. To find food, some whales must dive deep into the ocean. Sperm whales stay underwater up to two hours at a time, reaching depths of 10,000 feet (3,048 meters). How can whales stay down for so long?

YOU CAN SEE THE
BALEEN FILTER ON
THIS SOUTHERN
RIGHT WHALE AS
IT SLOWLY SWIMS
ALONG, FEEDING
AS IT GOES.

Their iron-rich blood carries a concentration of oxygen, and they store oxygen in their muscles, as well as in the lungs. This extra oxygen and a slowed-down heart-beat allow whales to stay underwater for long periods of time.

Sooner or later, all whales must come up for air. When a whale surfaces, it gives a powerful snort, spraying mist from its blowhole sometimes as high as 25 feet (8 meters).

At the surface, whales can be very playful. Right whales and sperm whales like to *breach*, or leap from the water, and land with a tremendous splash. Gray whales are known to *spy-hop*, or peek above the surface of the water. Other whales like to slap their tails against the water, which is known as *lobtailing*.

. . .
WHALE COMMUNICATION
THE CLICKS, WHISTLES, AND OTHER SOUNDS THAT WHALES MAKE AREN'T ONLY FOR ECHOLOCATION. SOME SCIENTISTS THINK THAT THEIR SOUNDS ARE USED FOR COMMUNICATION. INDEED, DIFFERENT WHALE GROUPS ARE KNOWN TO SING DIFFERENT SONGS. THE SONGS OF THE HUMPBACK WHALE WAS A RECORD ALBUM IN THE 1970S. IT IS THE ONLY HIT RECORDING EVER TO BE SUNG BY NONHUMANS.
. . .

THIS IS NOT A SEA MONSTER, BUT A FIN WHALE TAKING IN FRESH AIR BEFORE DIVING DEEP INTO THE OCEAN.

MANY WHALES, INCLUDING GRAY WHALES, LIKE TO BREACH. THIS GRAY WAS SPOTTED OFF THE COAST OF BAJA, CALIFORNIA.

4
THE LIFE OF A WHALE

Traveling is an important part of many whales' lives. Baleen whales are more likely to *migrate*, or travel long distances, twice a year, than toothed whales. Some whales, like the bowhead, migrate only short distances. Others, such as humpbacks and gray whales, migrate thousands of miles.

Why do these whales migrate so far? Most animals that migrate to warmer places are looking for food. Not baleen whales. They spend the summer eating in the Arctic. They have to fill up, because most of them won't eat at all in

BELUGA WHALES MIGRATE A VERY LONG DISTANCE TO GIVE BIRTH TO THEIR BABIES IN WARMER WATERS.

A SPERM WHALE POD. SPERM WHALES, LIKE MANY OTHER TOOTHED WHALES, SPEND MUCH OF THEIR TIME WANDERING THE OCEAN.

the winter. During the winter, they migrate to warmer waters and focus on breeding.

Breeding is done many ways. Many baleen whales gather in large groups. As many as three thousand gray whales meet every year during breeding season in the shallow lagoons of Baja California. Two males will pair off with one female. The primary male will mate first. The escort male will need to wait for his chance.

. . .

HOW DO WHALES NAVIGATE?
INDIVIDUALS IN A POD OF BALEEN WHALES CAN SCATTER OVER MANY MILES. HOW DO THESE WHALES COMMUNICATE? ONE ANSWER MAY BE THE **LOW-FREQUENCY** SOUNDS THAT WHALES BROADCAST THROUGH THE WATER. THESE SOUNDS CAN BE HEARD FOR HUNDREDS OF MILES. MANY SCIENTISTS THINK THAT LOW-FREQUENCY SOUNDS ARE USED FOR INTRAPOD COMMUNICATION, WHICH HELPS WHALES STAY TOGETHER AND FIND THEIR WAY DURING MIGRATION.

. . .

Some baleen whales must battle each other for the right to mate. Large groups of male humpbacks and right whales compete, charging and lunging at each other at breakneck speed to gain a female's favor.

Toothed whales often follow a different mating pattern. A single alpha, or lead, male sperm whale will join a group of females with whom he can mate. Meanwhile, the rest of the adult males travel in bachelor schools. Occasionally, these bachelors will be able to mate with females from a breeding school.

Female whales are typically pregnant for about a year. At birth, a blue whale calf may weigh as much as 3 tons. Drinking its mother's super-rich milk, a calf

UNLIKE OTHER TOOTHED WHALES, KILLER WHALE PODS DO NOT MAKE LONG MIGRATIONS. USUALLY, THEY GO WHEREVER PREY CAN BE FOUND.

gains 8 pounds (3.5 kilograms) of body weight each hour! The calf needs this weight because it will soon follow its mother on a long journey to arctic waters.

Baleen whales become independent of their mothers pretty quickly. The sei whale calf drinks its mother's milk for only six to seven months. Toothed whales stay close to their mothers for much longer. Sperm whales may nurse for twenty-four months.

Once they are grown, baleen whales do not stay very close to each other. Their pods are spread out over long distances. The blue whale, for example, often swims by itself or in pairs. Rarely is it found in larger groups. Toothed whale pods are much more tightly knit. These whales sometimes bond with each other for life. Killer whales can form pods of five to twenty-five whales. They swim together, hunt together, and even share their own language of clicks and whistles, which no other pod can understand.

The length of a whale's life varies widely. Some small whales live for only fifteen years. Larger whales

LIKE THE BABIES OF OTHER TOOTHED WHALES, BABY PILOT WHALES STAY CLOSE TO THEIR MOTHERS FOR A LONG TIME.

tend to live longer. Sei whales and blue whales live seventy years or more. Sperm whales live at least fifty years.

Toothed whales watch their young much more closely than baleen whales. Female sperm whales are known to baby-sit for one another within a pod. Each whale will take turns diving. While they dive, the other adult females take turns watching the babies.

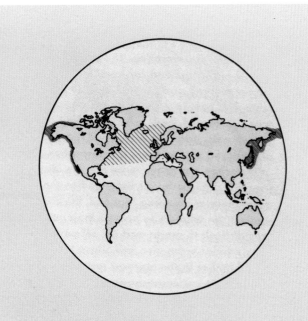

WHERE GRAY WHALES LIVE

 PAST HABITAT

 PRESENT HABITAT

Gray whales once lived throughout the northern Atlantic and Pacific Oceans. They now live only along the coasts of the Pacific. One group, the western gray whales, migrate between South Korea and the northern Siberian coast. The other group migrates between Baja California and the Bering Sea off Alaska and Siberia.

A MOTHER HUMP-
BACK AND HER
CALF. HUMPBACKS
DO NOT HAVE
STRONG TIES TO
THEIR PODS.
THIS MOTHER
AND CHILD
WILL SEPARATE
BEFORE LONG.

5

WHALES IN TODAY'S WORLD

Why do people hunt whales? In the past, whale meat was prized. Whale oil was even more valu-able. Some whale oils were actually worth their weight in gold. Products made from whales included lamp oil, umbrellas, corsets, and soap.

The Basques from Spain were among the ear-liest whalers. In the Middle Ages they hunted whales along the Atlantic coast. By the mid–1800s, whaling had become a major commercial indus-try. Each year, hundreds of ships set out from Nantucket, Massachusetts, on three– and four–year whaling voyages. Within a few decades, bowhead and right whales were almost *extinct*, or killed off.

A WHALE HUNT IN ALASKA. ONLY NATIVE PEOPLE SUCH AS THE INUIT ARE NOW ALLOWED TO KILL WHALES. THESE PEOPLE HAVE HUNTED WHALES FOR CENTURIES WITHOUT HURTING THE OVER-ALL POPULATION. IT WAS THE MASS WHALING BY EUROPEANS AND AMERICANS THAT LED TO THE NEAR EXTINCTION OF WHALES.

In the early twentieth century, whaling technology improved. Explosive harpoons and "floating factory" whaling ships killed many more whales—some 360,000 blue whales, 750,000 fin whales, and 400,000 sperm whales. The killing continued until many species, including the blue whale, had nearly disappeared. Finally, in 1986, the world's whaling countries got together and banned commercial whaling.

Today, many whale populations are threatened. Only a few hundred arctic bowheads, western grays, and northern right whales remain. Blue whales were almost completely wiped out. But they now appear to be recovering, as are other whale populations. Whales are still threatened by pollution and fishing, though. Pollution harms whales by harming the animals they feed on—shrimp, krill, and other ocean creatures. Fishing accidentally traps whales in large nets.

Some countries want to permit hunting whales again. Will whaling return? If it does, whalers will need to be smarter this time. Whales are one of the world's great treasures. People need to work together to make sure these treasures stay around forever.

. . .

HOW MANY WHALES ARE LEFT?

MILLIONS OF WHALES EXISTED IN THE PAST.
TODAY'S ESTIMATED POPULATIONS INCLUDE

· BLUE WHALES: 6,000 TO 14,000

· NORTHERN RIGHT WHALES: 300 TO 600

· SPERM WHALES: 300,000 TO 2,000,000

· HUMPBACK WHALES: 6,000 TO 9,000

· FIN WHALES: 20,000 TO 60,000

· GRAY WHALES: 15,000 TO 25,000

· NARWHAL WHALES: 25,000 TO 45,000

· KILLER WHALES: UNKNOWN

. . .

GRAY WHALES LIKE THIS ONE USED TO BE HUNTED FOR THEIR MEAT AND OIL. THEY ONCE LIVED IN THE NORTHERN ATLANTIC OCEAN, BUT CAN NOW BE FOUND ONLY IN THE PACIFIC OCEAN.

THE SIGHT OF A HUMPBACK WHALE BREACHING HIGH INTO THE AIR IS TRULY AWESOME. HUMPBACK WHALES APPEAR TO BE MAKING A COMEBACK. HOWEVER, HUMANS NEED TO BE CAREFUL NOT TO HARM THESE BEAUTIFUL CREATURES AND THEIR CETACEAN RELATIVES EVER AGAIN.

baleen: interlocking plates hanging from the upper jaw that whales use to strain food.

blowhole: a nostril that whales use for breathing.

blubber: a layer of fat that protects whales from losing heat.

breach: the act of leaping out of the water.

cetacean: a group of mammals that includes dolphins, porpoises, and whales.

cold–blooded: animals that get most of their body heat from the outside environment.

echolocation: the method by which whales use sound to locate things underwater.

extinct: when an entire species of animal is completely killed off.

filter feeder: an animal that takes in water and strains out food through a filter.

gills: organs through which water–dwelling animals breathe oxygen.

lob–tailing: when a whale slaps its tail against the water.

low-frequency sounds: very low sounds that can travel hundreds of miles underwater without fading out.

mammals: warm-blooded vertebrates (animals with backbones) that have body hair and give birth to live young that nurse on their mother's milk.

migrate: travel once a year to a distant spot to breed or feed.

pod: a group of whales that spends time together.

rorqual: fast, sleek baleen whales with throat grooves, including the blue whale, fin whale, and humpback whale.

species: a group of animals with similar features that are able to reproduce.

spy-hopping: when a whale lifts its head above the water.

warm-blooded: animals that burn food to create their own body heat.

BOOKS

Carwardine, Mark. *Whales, Dolphins, and Porpoises.* New York: Dorling Kindersley, 1995.

Clapham, Phil. *Whales of the World.* Stillwater, MN: Voyageur Press, 1997.

Ellis, Richard. *The Book of Whales.* New York: Knopf, 1985.

Leatherwood, Stephen and Randall R. Reeves. *The Sierra Club Handbook of Whales and Dolphins.* San Francisco: Sierra Club Books, 1983.

Papastavrou, Vassili. *Whale.* New York: Knopf, 1993.

Corrigan, Patricia. *The Whale Watcher's Guide:Whale-Watching Trips in North America.* Minneapolis, MN: NorthWord Press, 1999.

WEBSITES

The Whale Center of New England
www.whalecenter.org

American Cetacean Society
www.acsonline.org

The Evergreen Project: Whale Tales
http://mbgnet.mobot.org/salt/whale/

Hawaii Whale Research Foundation
www.hwrf.org/

Jaap's Marine Mammal Pages
http://ourworld.compuserve.com/homepages/jaap/

Pacific Whale Foundation
www.pacificwhale.org/

World Wildlife Fund — Endangered Species
www.worldwildlife.org/species/species.cfm?sectionid=193&newspaperid=21

Dan Greenberg has written numerous books for readers of all ages, on topics that range from science, to math, to baseball. His best known book series now has ten titles and includes *Comic Strip Math* and *Comic Strip Grammar*. Mr. Greenberg's favorite whale is the playful humpback.